For my parents ✤
who encouraged me to weave
the most delightful garden ... my imagination.

I love you dearly.
T.

For John ✤
Thank you for feeding my soul.
xoxo

P.S.
This book includes the heart and imagination
of a delightful team.
Thank you for being part of this journey.

Woven in Sunlight
A Garden Companion

Created by
Tracy Porter

Andrews McMeel
Publishing

Kansas City

WITH WRITING BY
DUKE CHRISTOFFERSEN,
PATRICK REGAN,
AND JOHN PORTER

PHOTOGRAPHY BY
DEBORAH FLETCHER
AND MAURA KOUTOUJIAN

ISBN: 0-8362-3179-1

Woven in Sunlight

A Garden Companion

with
Vivid
Colors

A garden is the result of the perfect relationship between art and artist. Gardeners fill soil, sow seeds, and create life for fruits and flowers, making sure they have water, sunlight and a caring hand to help them grow. The fruits and flowers return the gift, nourishing their gardeners, in both body and spirit. A garden is a symbol, a constant reminder of nature's glory. It is an un-changing masterpiece, saturated the textures, shapes and hues that painters and sculptors have striven to recreate.

If I had
but two loaves
of bread, I would
sell one of them
and buy white
hyacinths to feed
my soul.
-the Koran

I sit contentedly upon a rather large stone in the corner of my garden. Mixed within chive, rosemary, and sage are flowers of color with no obvious purpose other than their magnificent beauty. As I sit, the quiet buzzing of a hummingbird freezes me. Floating from flower to flower, this weightless bird, no bigger than my thumb, carries me beyond all my everydays, and I am lost in the courtship of this fairy-like creature and the blossoms full with nectar. Soon, I will return, but for now, my spirit is revived and the garden soothes my soul.

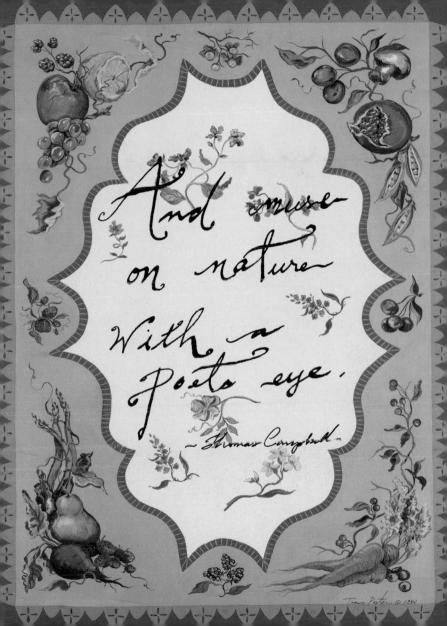

And muse
on nature
with a
Poet's eye.

~ Thomas Campbell

By viewing Nature, Nature's handmaid Art,

*Makes mighty things from
small beginnings grow.*
        –John Dryden

Now the summer came to pass

and flowers through the grass

joyously sprang,

while all the tribes of birds sang.

—Walter von der Vogelweid

*F*lower in the
crannied wall,
I pluck you out
of the crannies,
I hold you
here, root and all,
in my hand, Little Flower—
but if I could understand what you are,
root and all, and all in all, I should
know what God and man is.

— *Alfred, Lord Tennyson*

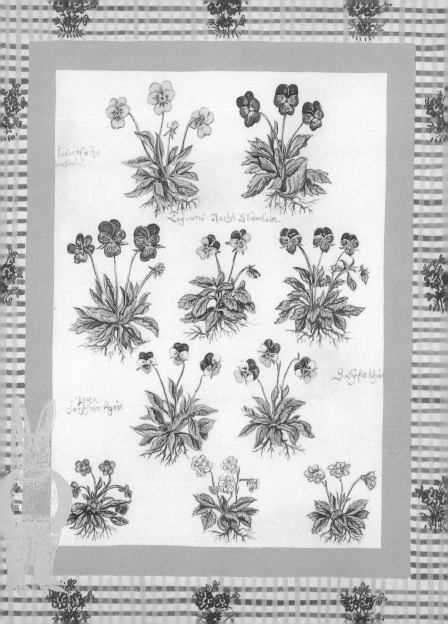

I like to walk about amidst the beautiful things that adorn the world.

— George Santayana

Down our long driveway, across the road and stretching as far as the eye could see was a cornfield that, in mid-summer, became a garden of our adventures. We would run between the rows, playing games and hiding. The lush aroma of ripened corn often slowed our hectic pace, and these thick, rich smells made us miss our tall fields, all the more when winter erased them each year. But we knew that spring would soon come again and, with it, the rebirth of the garden of our adventures.

All nature wears

one universal grin.

— Henry
Fielding

Nothing is more completely the child of art than a garden.

–Sir Walter Scott

Selangste Rammel
mit langen bleumlanen anutragendt

L Bellone Perennsen gespeicendt fetten

Perfianifue Silien Fenghnotli le

h that at times it paralyzes me

Tracy Porter

Show me your garden
and I shall tell you
what you are.

Miguel de Cervantes

The creative process excites me so r

The windows of my soul

I throw wide open to the sun.
– John Greenleaf Whittier

In his garden every man may be his own artist without apology or explanation. Here is one spot where each may experience the "romance of possibility."

—Louise Beebe Wilder

The poetry of the earth is never dead.

– John Keats

I Always invite fairies into
my gardens ... and my imagination
They stir my thoughts, they have
tea on the Laps of my pansies
They nap on the tongue
of my foxglove

They
powder their noses with
pollen ... Ah how they
delight my senses.

No amount of skillful invention can replace the essential element of imagination.
— *Edward Hopper*

There are Times
When a dream
delicious

Steals in a

Musing hour.

— John Boyle O'Reilly

I have a very loose interpretation of what a garden is. Each year, my mother would plant hundreds, maybe thousands, of daffodils in a field between the pond and our house. Each spring, the field would come alive in an explosion of yellow! What a garden! On the other side of the pond, my father planted irises. (And how our two mute swans dined delightfully on my father's hard work!)

Each year as the blazing daffodil grew weary, dad's irises would take up the charge in a burst of proud purple.

Gather ye rosebuds while ye may, Old Time is still a-flying, And this same flower that smiles today Tomorrow will be dying. — Robert Herrick

*T*o see a world

in a grain of sand

And a heaven in a wild flower,

Hold infinity in

the palm of your hand

And eternity in an hour.

— *William Blake*

Come forsythia

and hyacinth

join in glad refrain

with iris, squill

and columbine

for spring

has come again.

BEAUTY IN OUR MEMORY.

THERE IS ALWAYS ROOM FOR

Mom and Grandma, 1948
Nuits St. George, France
In the orchard.

Grandma Lucy and Tata,
1922 in the bois de bologne, Paris

Grandma and Grandpa Schaberg,
1936...picnicing in the park.

Langage des fleurs

ŒILLET
tendre amitié

LIERRE
"je meurs où
je m'attache"

ROSE
tendre amour

Annette, 1946, visiting gardens with Odette.

Who can forget those days when to announce the appearance of a bud ... or the perfection of a full-blown peony, was glory enough for one morning. —Joseph Breck

I know a little garden close,

Set thick with lily and red rose,

Where I would wander if I might

From dewy morn to dewy night.
—William Morris

Nobody sees a flower — really — it is so small it takes time — we haven't time and to see takes time, like to have a friend takes time.

— *Georgia O'Keefe*

Each day at dawn, a grand opera begins in my backyard. I've the finest seat in the house— an ancient piece of flagstone in the center of my garden. From it, I regard an ensemble of morning glories. Their proud cobalt trumpets herald the arrival of the sun, slung low in a hazy mid-August sky. They follow in rapt attention as the blazing conductor of day moves in a rising arc toward a moment in late morning when the light and warmth that roused them, gains strength enough to overwhelm. The day's overture done, they quietly lower their horns while on the opposite end of the garden, a single noble sunflower groggily shakes off sleep and slowly raises its head for a soaring aria that will last until the sun drops his final baton of light.

Shall I sing of happy hours numbered by opening and closing flowers? — Hartley Coleridge

Flowers are made
to seduce the senses:
Fragrance, form, colour.

—Heidi Dodde

The greatest thing
a human soul ever does
in this world is to see something.
...To see clearly is poetry,
prophecy, and religion,
all in one.

— John Ruskin
Modern Painters

What a pity! Flowers can utter no sound! A singing rose, a whispering violet, a murmuring honeysuckle — oh, what a rare and exquisite miracle would there be!

—Henry Ward Beecher

I know a bank whereon the wild thyme blows,
　　Where oxlips and the nodding violet grows
Quite over-canopied with luscious woodbine,
　　With sweet musk-roses, and with eglantine:
There sleeps Titania some time of the night,
　　Lull'd in these flowers with dances and delight;
And there the snake throws her enamell'd skin,
　　Weed wide enough to wrap a fairy in.

- William Shakespeare,
　　A Midsummer-Night's Dream

Some people like to make
a little garden out of life
and walk down a path.
— Jean Anouilh